NOV – 2013

INVESTIGATING
PLATE
TECTONICS,
EARTHQUAKES,
AND VOLCANOES

INVESTIGATING PLATE TECTONICS, EARTHQUAKES, AND VOLCANOES

EDITED BY MICHAEL ANDERSON

Britannica®
Educational Publishing
IN ASSOCIATION WITH

ROSEN
EDUCATIONAL SERVICES

Published in 2012 by Britannica Educational Publishing
(a trademark of Encyclopædia Britannica, Inc.)
in association with Rosen Educational Services, LLC
29 East 21st Street, New York, NY 10010.

Distributed exclusively by Rosen Educational Services.
For a listing of additional Britannica Educational Publishing titles, call toll free (800) 237-9932.

First Edition

Britannica Educational Publishing
Michael I. Levy: Executive Editor, Encyclopædia Britannica
J.E. Luebering: Director, Core Reference Group, Encyclopædia Britannica
Adam Augustyn: Assistant Manager, Encyclopædia Britannica

Anthony L. Green: Editor, Compton's by Britannica
Michael Anderson: Senior Editor, Compton's by Britannica
Sherman Hollar: Associate Editor, Compton's by Britannica

Marilyn L. Barton: Senior Coordinator, Production Control
Steven Bosco: Director, Editorial Technologies
Lisa S. Braucher: Senior Producer and Data Editor
Yvette Charboneau: Senior Copy Editor
Kathy Nakamura: Manager, Media Acquisition

Rosen Educational Services
Alexandra Hanson-Harding: Editor
Nelson Sá: Art Director
Cindy Reiman: Photography Manager
Matthew Cauli: Designer, Cover Design
Introduction by Alexandra Hanson-Harding

Library of Congress Cataloging-in-Publication Data

Investigating plate tectonics, earthquakes, and volcanoes / edited by Michael Anderson.—1st ed.
    p. cm.—(Introduction to earth science)
"In association with Britannica Educational Publishing, Rosen Educational Services."
Includes bibliographical references and index.
ISBN 978-1-61530-504-9 (lib. bdg.)
1. Earthquakes—Juvenile literature. 2. Volcanoes—Juvenile literature. 3. Plate tectonics—Juvenile
literature. I. Anderson, Michael, 1972-
QE521.3.I58 2012
551.22—dc22

2010050581

Manufactured in the United States of America

On the cover, page 3: Lava flows down a mountain during a volcanic eruption. *Shutterstock.com*

Interior background ©www.istockphoto.com/Beboy_ltd

CONTENTS

The tropical island of Java, Indonesia, has sweeping beaches, lush landscapes, and majestic mountains. But in late 2010 the eruption of Java's Mount Merapi volcano made parts of the island an ugly nightmare. Huge gas clouds and fiery rocks spewed high into the air. Glowing lava snaked down the mountainside. Showers of ash draped homes and fields in ghostly gray. Later, search and rescue teams hunted for survivors but found mostly bodies, some charred, caught in mid-flight. In the end, hundreds of people were killed. This powerful eruption is just one illustration of why many Earth scientists focus on the study of plate tectonics.

Plate tectonics is the modern theory of the movement of Earth's outer shell, or lithosphere. The lithosphere consists of the planet's rocky surface layer, called the crust, and the solid outermost layer of the mantle beneath. The lithosphere is broken into about a dozen large plates and several smaller ones. The plates float on a much hotter layer of partially molten rock called the asthenosphere, which is also part of the mantle. The asthenosphere slowly churns, driven to movement by radioactive heating of the planet's core. This churning causes the plates of the lithosphere to move at a rate of about 2 to 4 inches (5 to 10 centimeters) a year.

Thick smoke rises from the Mount Merapi volcano on the island of Java, Indonesia, on Oct. 26, 2010. **AFP/Getty Images**

At their edges, the plates interact with each other in one of three ways: they converge, diverge, or slip past each other. When two oceanic plates converge, or come together, the older, denser plate slides under the younger plate. When oceanic crust meets denser continental crust, the oceanic crust slides underneath. In other places plates diverge, or spread apart. In the middle of the oceans, long ridges form where plates diverge. Magma, or molten rock, rises from the mantle and fills in the gap, creating new seafloor. On the continents, diverging plates create troughs called rift valleys. The most extensive of these is East Africa's Great Rift Valley.

Along some boundaries two plates neither converge nor diverge; instead they slide past each other along fractures in the crust. These fractures are called transform faults. The plates sometimes stick, causing a buildup of pressure that may be released in the form of an earthquake. The sudden and sometimes violent shaking caused by earthquakes kills about 10,000 people a year. Approximately 80 percent of the world's earthquakes occur in the Ring of Fire, a belt circling the Pacific Ocean that traces the boundaries of tectonic plates.

The Pacific Ring of Fire is also the site of about 90 percent of the world's volcanoes.

Volcanoes are vents in Earth's surface through which molten rock, gas, and ash erupt. The name is perhaps more commonly used for the mountains formed by the buildup of material erupted from these vents. The most prevalent type of volcano is the stratovolcano, a steep, cone-shaped mountain made up of layers of rock fragments and hardened lava. Japan's Mount Fuji is a classic example of a stratovolcano. Shield volcanoes are another common type. Typical of Hawaii, they are dome-shaped mountains formed by the accumulation of broad lava flows.

Volcanoes, earthquakes, mountain building—these fundamental phenomena of Earth science can all be explained by plate tectonics. The theory provides invaluable insight into the processes that have shaped the face of the planet over many millions of years. But understanding the movements of Earth's crust can have more immediate and tangible benefits as well. For instance, experts are using technology to try to predict earthquakes and volcanic eruptions and to create buildings that can withstand the deadly force of earthquakes. Their work may be able to help more people survive tectonic catastrophes like the explosion of Mount Merapi.

CHAPTER 1
PLATE TECTONICS

The modern theory of the motions of Earth's outer layers is called plate tectonics. It provides a framework for understanding many of Earth's features, such as mountains, earthquakes, and volcanoes, as well as the distribution of fossils and the ages of rocks. It also helps scientists reconstruct ancient climates and continental configurations.

BASICS OF THE THEORY

In 1912 the German meteorologist Alfred Wegener proposed that the continents had once been joined as a gigantic landmass called Pangea (also spelled Pangaea). According to this theory, called continental drift, the supercontinent long ago broke into pieces (the present continents), which have since drifted to their current positions. At the time, many geologists rejected Wegener's ideas, partly because he had no convincing explanation why continents would move.

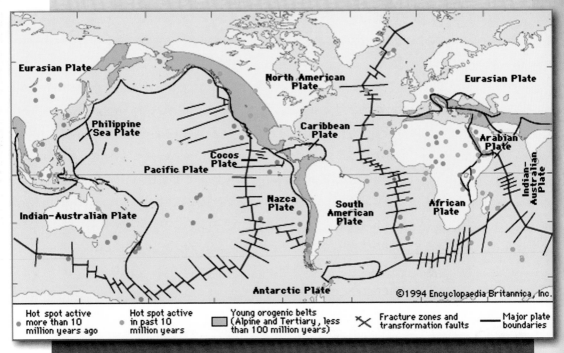

Hot spot active
● more than 10
million years ago

Hot spot active
● in past 10
million years

▢ Young orogenic belts
(Alpine and Tertiary, less
than 100 million years)

✕ Fracture zones and
transformation faults

— Major plate
boundaries

The map shows the principal tectonic plates that make up Earth's crust. Also located are orogenic belts, or great mountain ranges, that have been produced comparatively recently at the boundaries of converging plates. The hot spots locate sites where plumes of hot mantle material are upwelling beneath the plates. **Encyclopædia Britannica, Inc.**

Since then, geologists have developed a better picture of Earth's internal structure. The surface layer is a crust of solid rock, the thickness of which ranges from just 3 miles (5 kilometers) in parts of the ocean bottom to about 45 miles (75 kilometers) in some continental areas. Below the crust is the denser rock of the mantle, on which the

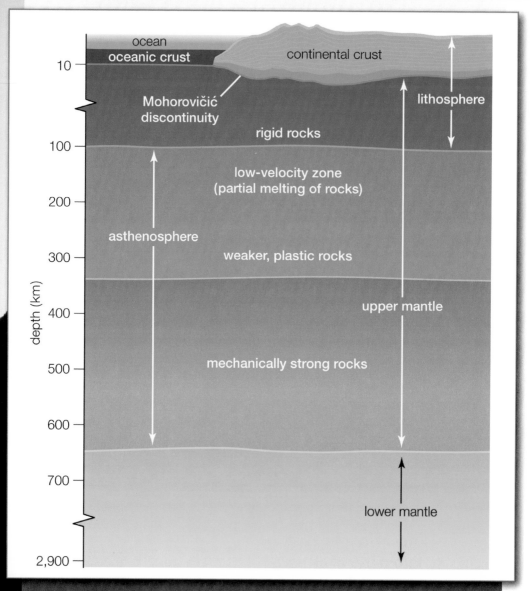

A cross section shows Earth's outer layers subdivided according to their physical properties. The crust and the uppermost part of the mantle form the rigid lithosphere. Below that is a partly molten zone, which overlies a more rigid zone. Encyclopædia Britannica, Inc.

crust effectively floats. The mantle extends to a depth of about 1,800 miles (2,900 kilometers), where temperatures reach roughly 6,700 °F (3,700 °C). Below the mantle is Earth's core, made largely of iron and nickel. The outer part of the core is liquid, the motions of which are believed to create Earth's magnetic field. The innermost core, though extremely hot, is solid because of the extreme pressure.

Much of what is known about Earth's internal structure comes from the study of vibrations called seismic waves, which result from earthquakes. The waves travel through Earth's interior and reflect or bend upon encountering changes in the density of the rock. One type of seismic wave is absorbed if it enters liquid. From this, scientists have discovered a partially molten zone in the mantle, between about 50 and 200 miles (80 and 350 kilometers) below the surface. This layer, called the asthenosphere, allows the uppermost mantle and crust—together called the lithosphere—to slide across the top of it. Earth's lithosphere is broken into about a dozen large pieces (plus some smaller ones), called plates. The edges of these plates do not necessarily correspond to the boundaries of continents or

ALFRED WEGENER AND CONTINENTAL DRIFT

Alfred Wegener, the originator of the continental drift theory, was born in Berlin, Germany, on Nov. 1, 1880. The son of a director of an orphanage, he received his doctorate in astronomy from the University of Berlin in 1905. During this time he became interested in meteorology and geology. Wegener went on four expeditions to Greenland and was considered a specialist on the territory. He taught meteorology at Marburg and Hamburg and was a professor of meteorology and geophysics at the University of Graz from 1924 to 1930. He died during his last expedition to Greenland in 1930.

Like some other scientists before him, Wegener became impressed with the similarity in the coastlines of eastern South America and western Africa, which appear that they would fit together like pieces of a jigsaw puzzle. He was not the first to speculate that those lands had once been joined together or that all the present-day continents had formed a single large mass, or supercontinent. However, other scientists had explained the separation of the modern continents as having resulted from the sinking of large portions of the supercontinent

to form the Atlantic and Indian oceans. Wegener, in contrast, proposed that Pangea broke apart and that its parts had slowly moved thousands of miles apart over long periods of geologic time. His term for this movement was *continental displacement*, which gave rise to the term *continental drift*.

oceans. For example, the North American Plate includes the western half of the North Atlantic Ocean's seafloor.

Scientists are now almost certain that Wegener's Pangea existed. It probably started to break apart from about 240 million to 200 million years ago after having been assembled from earlier continents only a few tens of millions of years earlier. It now seems that earlier incarnations of Pangea may have occurred, as part of a roughly 400-million-year cycle of the breakup and reassembly of supercontinents.

PLATE MOVEMENTS

The way the plates interact at their margins depends on whether the crust forming the top of the plate (at the point of contact) is oceanic or continental. Continental

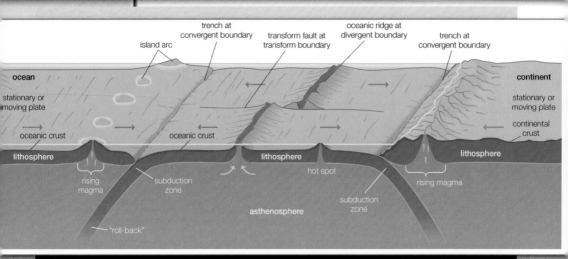

island arc
trench at convergent boundary
transform fault at transform boundary
oceanic ridge at divergent boundary
trench at convergent boundary
ocean
stationary or moving plate
oceanic crust
lithosphere
rising magma
subduction zone
lithosphere
hot spot
asthenosphere
subduction zone
continent
stationary or moving plate
continental crust
lithosphere
rising magma
"roll-back"
oceanic crust

A diagram shows several kinds of interactions at plate boundaries, including convergent boundaries where oceanic crust meets oceanic crust, at left, and where oceanic crust meets continental crust, at right. Divergent and transform boundaries associated with seafloor spreading are shown in the center. **Encyclopædia Britannica, Inc.**

crust—made largely of granite—is less dense than oceanic crust—made largely of basalt. As the plates move, they may converge, or come together; diverge, or spread apart; or slide past each other along fractures called transform faults.

CONVERGENCE

Generally, if two plates are converging, the denser plate will be forced under, or subducted beneath, the less dense one. The subducted

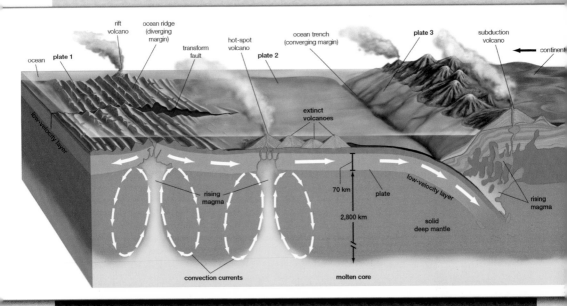

A diagram shows the relationship between volcanic activity and Earth's tectonic plates. Different kinds of volcanoes are formed in different ways. Stratovolcanoes tend to form at subduction zones, or convergent plate margins, where an oceanic plate slides beneath a continental plate and contributes to the rise of magma to the surface. At rift zones, or divergent margins, shield volcanoes tend to form as two oceanic plates pull slowly apart and magma effuses upward through the gap. Volcanoes are not generally found at strike-slip zones, where two plates slide laterally past each other. "Hot spot" volcanoes may form where plumes of lava rise from deep within the mantle to Earth's crust far from any plate margins. Encyclopædia Britannica, Inc.

crust is eventually destroyed. This happens when oceanic crust meets continental crust and when oceanic crust meets oceanic crust. For example, the eastward-moving Nazca

Plate, under the southeastern Pacific Ocean, is being subducted under the westward-moving South American Plate. The denser oceanic crust is thrust down into the mantle, causing it to melt and produce magma (molten rock). The magma and gases rise to the surface and are vented through the western crust of South America, forming the volcanoes of the Andes Mountains. Sometimes pieces of the descending plate break off and stick in place deep underground for a time before suddenly moving, causing powerful earthquakes. Also, a deep ocean trench forms just offshore, where the oceanic crust is being forced downward.

If two oceanic plates converge, subduction of one under the other may produce an arc of volcanic islands. The Mariana Islands of the western Pacific Ocean were formed this way.

Two blocks of continental crust may converge as well. The resulting pressure can deform the crust. If one block is denser, that block may slide under the other, mainly lifting the other plate rather than sinking too much itself. A good example of this is the convergence of the northward moving Indo-Australian Plate with the Eurasian Plate. As India meets Asia, the collision produces the highest mountain range on Earth—the Himalayas.

DIVERGENCE

The destruction of crust that occurs with subduction must be compensated by the creation of crust elsewhere. This occurs where plates are diverging from each other at oceanic ridges, such as in the middle of the Atlantic Ocean. There, rising magma fills in what would otherwise be a widening crack, producing new seafloor. Undersea volcanoes and crust expanded by heating have produced a long undersea ridge, but with a rift in the middle where the plates are separating. This process is known as seafloor spreading. Shallow earthquakes are common at oceanic ridges, as the seafloor fractures, fills in, and fractures again.

Divergence can also happen on continents, producing fractures called rift valleys. A modern example is the East African Rift System, also called the Great Rift Valley. Over millions of years the continental crust may separate completely, with the area between flooding with water to become a new ocean.

GREAT RIFT VALLEY

The longest rift on Earth's surface, the Great Rift Valley is a long, deep depression with steep, wall-like cliffs, extending from Jordan in southwestern Asia southward through Africa to Mozambique. The rift has a total length of approximately 4,000 miles (6,400 kilometers) and an average width of 30 to 40 miles (50 to

65 kilometers). It is a continental extension of the midoceanic ridge system, a generally submerged mountain range encircling the globe. The valley is least eroded, and therefore most conspicuous, in eastern Africa, where it is also known as the East African Rift Valley.

The floor of the valley is frequently below sea level. The topography is varied and includes lakes, volcanoes, desert, and plains. The cliffs that border the valley, known as escarpments, rise an average of 2,000 to 3,000 feet (600 to 900 meters) above the valley floor. In some places, however, such as in the Mau Escarpment in Kenya, these walls rise as much as 9,000 feet (2,700 meters) above the valley floor and provide some of the valley's most spectacular scenery. Many of Africa's highest mountains—including Mount Kilimanjaro, Mount Kenya, and Mount Margherita—are in ranges fronting the Rift Valley.

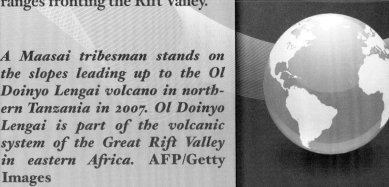

A Maasai tribesman stands on the slopes leading up to the Ol Doinyo Lengai volcano in northern Tanzania in 2007. Ol Doinyo Lengai is part of the volcanic system of the Great Rift Valley in eastern Africa. AFP/Getty Images

Section of the San Andreas Fault in the Carrizo Plain, western California. U.S. Geological Survey

TRANSFORM FAULTS

In some places, plates slide past each other laterally along fractures in the crust. These places are called transform faults. The plates stick and then occasionally slip, producing earthquakes. Most transform faults are found on the seafloor along the undersea mountain chains called oceanic ridges, but the faults also occur on continents, such as the San Andreas Fault in California. As plates move past each other along transform faults, crust is neither destroyed nor created.

CAUSES OF PLATE MOTIONS

The causes of plate motions are not completely understood, but a major factor appears to be giant convection cells (churning motions) in the mantle. Currents of hot material rise while currents of colder material sink, forming roughly circular cells—a common pattern of heat circulation that can also be seen in a pot of boiling water. In this way, the planet's interior redistributes heat resulting from the decay of long-lived radioactive elements such as uranium. Plates may also be pulled along by a subducting margin as the dense crust sinks into the mantle. There is

Coal and petrified wood found on Antarctica show that plants once lived there. Maria Stenzel/National Geographic Image Collection/ Getty Images

evidence that some old plate fragments may have sunk almost to the core.

FURTHER SUCCESSES

In addition to accounting for earthquakes, volcanoes, mountains, and oceanic ridges, plate tectonics and the resulting drift of continents have explained many curious facts. Very similar groups of fossils have been found far apart, probably carried away from each other when continents split. Coal in Antarctica formed from forests that grew there when that land was much closer to the Equator. Evidence of glaciers in Africa points to a time when Africa was part of an ancient continent near the South Pole.

Also, many rocks retain a record of how the planet's magnetic field was oriented when they formed. Earth's magnetic field periodically reverses polarity, so that the north and south magnetic poles essentially switch. Bands of rocks with alternating magnetic polarity on the western Atlantic seafloor have corresponding bands on the eastern Atlantic seafloor. These matching bands are neatly explained by seafloor spreading carrying fresh rock, magnetized by Earth's magnetic field at the time, off in both directions.

Continental crust, which is rarely subducted, contains rocks up to 4 billion years old. On the other hand, no oceanic crust has been found over 200 million years old—because, according to plate tectonics, the denser oceanic crust is subducted, destroyed, and recycled. Finally, by using methods including radio telescopes stationed on different continents and Global Positioning System (GPS) satellites, scientists have measured plate motions directly. Typical speeds are 2 to 4 inches (5 to 10 centimeters) per year, matching well with long-term trends expected from the theory.

CHAPTER 2
THE NATURE OF EARTHQUAKES

The sudden shaking of the ground that occurs when masses of rock change position below Earth's surface is called an earthquake. The shifting of the rock releases a great amount of energy, sending out shock waves that travel through the rock and cause the ground to shake. These shock waves—called seismic waves by Earth scientists—may be powerful enough to alter the surface, thrusting up cliffs and opening great cracks in the ground.

Earthquakes occur most often along geologic faults, which are fractures in the rocks of Earth's crust. Along faults, the rock masses on opposite sides of the fracture strain against each other and sometimes "slip," causing an earthquake. The major fault lines of the world are located at the fringes of the huge tectonic plates that make up the crust.

Earthquakes, called temblors by scientists, occur almost continuously. Fortunately, most of them can be detected only by sensitive instruments called seismographs.

Others are felt as small tremors. Some of the rest, however, cause major catastrophes. A very great earthquake usually occurs at least once a year in some part of the world. According to long-term data of the United States Geological Survey, on average about 10,000 people die each year as a result of

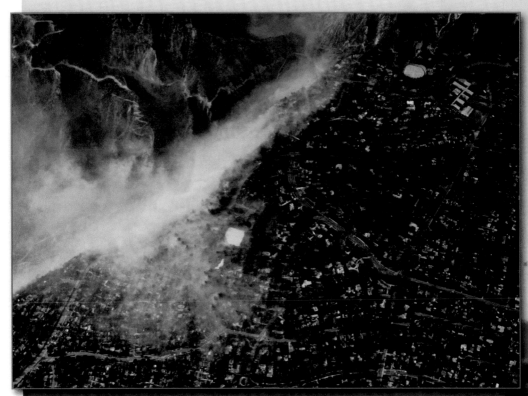

An aerial view of the La Cañada foothills near Los Angeles, Calif., on Oct. 1, 1987, during the Whittier Narrows earthquake, which measured 5.9 on the Richter scale. This image is one of the few still photographs ever taken of any earthquake while it is taking place. George Rose/ Getty Images

earthquakes. Humankind has long been concerned about earthquake hazards. The oldest chronicle comes from the Chinese as early as the Shang Dynasty more than 3,000 years ago.

CAUSES

Most of the worst earthquakes are associated with changes in the shape of Earth's outermost shell, particularly the crust. These earthquakes are generated by the rapid release of strain energy that is stored within the rocks of the crust. A small proportion of earthquakes are associated with human activity. Dynamite or atomic explosions, for example, can sometimes cause mild quakes. The injection of liquid wastes deep into the ground and the pressures resulting from holding vast amounts of water in reservoirs behind large dams can also trigger minor earthquakes.

The strongest and most destructive quakes are associated with ruptures of the crust, which are known as faults. Although faults are present in most regions of the world, earthquakes are not associated with all of them. Pressures from within Earth strain the tectonic plates that make up the crust. The strain builds until suddenly the plates move along faults, thereby releasing energy. The plates slip and slide in opposite directions along the fracture in the rock, shaking the ground above. The plates may move up and down, sideways, or vertically and horizontally. On Earth's surface displacement of the ground may vary from a few inches to many feet (or several centimeters to many meters). Some fault lines appear on the surface.

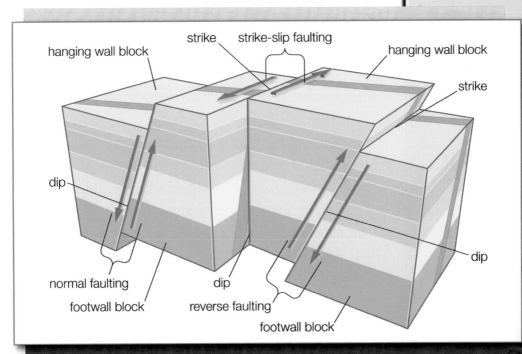

Types of faulting in tectonic earthquakes. In normal and reverse faulting, rock masses slip vertically past each other. In strike-slip faulting, the rocks slip past each other horizontally. **Encyclopædia Britannica, Inc.**

SHOCK WAVES

The shifting rock in an earthquake causes shock waves—called seismic waves—to spread through the rock in all directions. In a great earthquake shocks may be felt by people thousands of miles or kilometers away from the center. Seismographs can pick up the waves on the other side of the world.

There are two broad classes of seismic waves: body waves and surface waves. Body waves travel within the body of Earth. They include P, or primary, waves and S, or secondary, waves. P waves spread in the crust from the point of rupture, which is called the focus of the earthquake. The point on Earth's surface immediately above the focus is termed the epicenter of an earthquake. P waves alternately compress and expand the rock through which they pass and vibrate in the same direction in which the waves travel. S waves vibrate at right angles to the direction of wave travel. These secondary waves are the "shake" waves that move particles up and down or from side to side. The speed of S waves is always less than that of P waves. By comparing the arrival times of both P waves and S waves at seismological observatories, scientists can determine the location of an earthquake many thousands of miles away.

After both P and S waves have moved through the body of Earth, they are followed by two types of surface waves, which travel along Earth's surface. These are named Love and Rayleigh waves, after the scientists who identified them. Because of their larger amplitude, surface waves are responsible for much of the destructive shaking that occurs far from the epicenter. Surface waves, which travel more slowly than body waves, are the most powerful shock waves.

EFFECTS

Earthquakes often cause dramatic changes at Earth's surface. In addition to the ground movements, other surface effects include changes in the flow of groundwater, landslides, and mudflows. Earthquakes can do significant damage to buildings, bridges, pipelines, railways, embankments, dams, and other structures.

Earthquakes can lead to devastating fires. Fire produced the greatest property loss following the 1906 San Francisco earthquake, when 521 blocks in the city center burned uncontrollably for three days. Fire also

Crowds watch the fires set off by the earthquake in San Francisco in 1906, in a photo by Arnold Genthe. **Library of Congress, Washington, D.C.**

followed the 1923 Tokyo earthquake, causing much damage and hardship for the citizens.

TSUNAMIS

Underwater earthquakes can cause giant waves called tsunamis. Violent shaking of the seafloor produces waves that spread over the ocean surface in ever-widening circles.

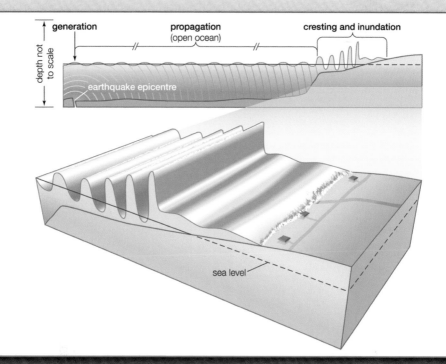

After being generated by an undersea earthquake or landslide, a tsunami may propagate unnoticed over vast reaches of open ocean before cresting in shallow water and inundating a coastline. Encyclopædia Britannica, Inc.

HISTORICAL TSUNAMIS

The deadliest tsunami in recorded history occurred in the Indian Ocean in December 2004. It was generated by an extremely large earthquake off the northwest coast of the Indonesian island of Sumatra. The tsunami devastated the islands and coasts of more than 10 countries in southern Asia and eastern Africa. The waves washed away entire

villages and killed more than 200,000 people. The death toll was the highest in Indonesia, Sri Lanka, India, and Thailand.

Other large tsunamis of recent history include one that ravaged the northwestern coast of Papua New Guinea in 1998, killing more than 2,100 people, and one that occurred in 1976 in the Philippines, killing about 8,000 people. Another major earthquake-generated tsunami took place in Chile in 1960. With a magnitude of 9.5, the earthquake was the largest ever recorded. The tsunami it generated was responsible for about 2,000 deaths along the Chile-Peru coast. After devastating the coastline of South America, the tsunami traveled for 15 hours across the Pacific to Hilo, Hawaii, claiming an additional 61 lives, and for 22 hours to Japan, killing another 122 people.

A fishing boat rests on a street as villagers return to Nam Kem, Thailand, a few days after a powerful tsunami swept the coast on Dec. 26 , 2004. **Romeo Gacad/AFP/Getty Images**

In deep water a tsunami can travel as fast as 500 miles (800 kilometers) per hour. By the time a tsunami reaches shore, it has gained tremendous size and power, reaching heights as great as 100 feet (30 meters). Tsunamis can be catastrophic, with the potential to wipe out coastal settlements.

OCCURRENCE

Most earthquakes take place on one of two great earthquake belts that girdle the world. The belts coincide with the more recently formed mountain ranges and with belts of volcanic activity. One earthquake belt circles the Pacific Ocean along the mountainous west coasts of North and South America and runs through the island areas of Asia. It is estimated that 80 percent of the energy released in earthquakes comes from this belt, which is called the Circum-Pacific Belt or the Ring of Fire.

A second, less active belt passes between Europe and North Africa through the Mediterranean region. It then runs eastward through Asia and joins the Ring of Fire in the East Indies. The energy released in earthquakes in this belt is about 15 percent of the world total. There are also striking connected

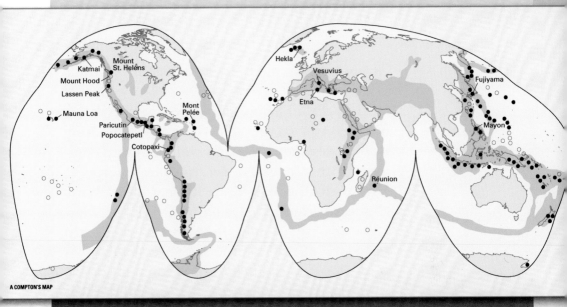

A COMPTON'S MAP

Earthquake zones around the world are marked in red. Black dots show active volcanoes and open dots dead zones. **Encyclopædia Britannica, Inc.**

belts of seismic activity, mainly along mid-oceanic ridges—including those in the Arctic Ocean, the Atlantic Ocean, and the western Indian Ocean—and along the Great Rift Valley of East Africa.

The focus of an earthquake may occur from quite close to the surface down to a maximum depth of about 430 miles (700 kilometers). More than 75 percent of the seismic energy produced each year, however, is released by shallow-focus earthquakes—that is, quakes with foci less than about 40 miles

RING OF FIRE

Around the boundaries of the Pacific tectonic plate are many active volcanoes and frequent earthquakes. The presence of numerous volcanoes has caused this zone to be called the Ring of Fire. Earthquakes, however, are more common in this belt than are volcanic eruptions. For much of its length the Ring of Fire follows chains of island arcs such as Tonga and New Hebrides, the Philippines, Japan, the Kuril Islands, and the Aleutians, or arc-shaped features, such as the Andes Mountains of South America. Deep ocean trenches bound the belt on the oceanic side; continental landmasses lie behind. The Ring of Fire is the source of approximately 80 percent of the world's shallow-focus earthquakes and virtually all deep-focus earthquakes.

(60 kilometers) deep. Most parts of the world experience at least occasional shallow-focus earthquakes. About 12 percent of the total energy released in earthquakes comes from intermediate earthquakes—those with foci ranging from about 40 to 200 miles (60 to 300 kilometers) deep. About 3 percent of the total energy comes from deeper earthquakes. The deeper-focus earthquakes commonly occur in Benioff zones, which dip down into

the mantle at places where two tectonic plates converge. A Benioff zone extends down along the plate that is being subducted.

Even though scientists are in general agreement that the regions of greatest tectonic instability coincide with the marginal zones of slowly moving plates, it must not be assumed that major earthquakes occur only along plate margins. Severe earthquakes occur on rare occasions with equally destructive force in zones of weakness within the plates.

CHAPTER 3

THE STUDY OF EARTHQUAKES

L ittle was understood about earthquakes until the emergence of seismology at the beginning of the 20th century. Seismology, which involves the scientific study of all aspects of earthquakes, has yielded answers to such long-standing questions as why and how earthquakes occur.

MEASUREMENT

A seismograph records the pattern of shock waves caused by an earthquake. Seismographs are equipped with electromagnetic sensors that translate ground motions into electrical changes, which are processed and recorded by the instrument. A record produced by a seismograph on a display screen or paper printout is called a seismogram.

Most seismographs use a pendulum. As the ground moves during an earthquake, so does the pendulum. The seismograph records the motion of pendulum relative to the motion of the ground. Early mechanical seismographs

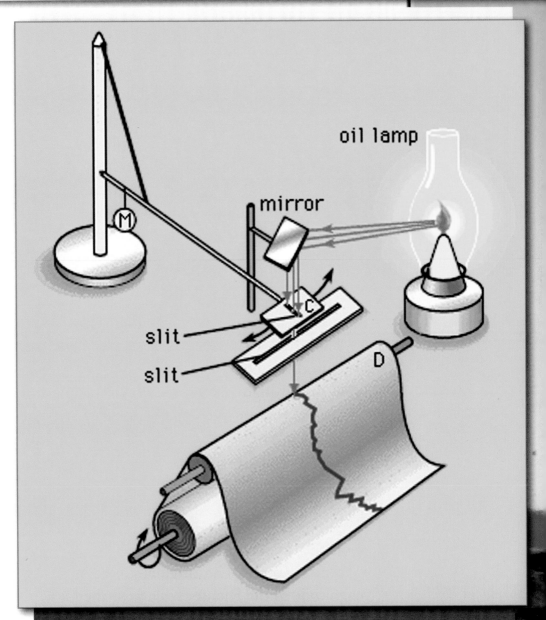

oil lamp

mirror

M

C

slit

slit

D

*Horizontal pendulum seismograph, as invented by English seismologist John Milne in 1880. From **Bulletin of the Seismological Society of America** (1969), vol. 59, no. 1, p. 212*

had a heavy pendulum and recorded the wave patterns by scratching a line on a revolving drum of paper. Later instruments used a mirror that was moved by the motion of the pendulum; light reflected by the mirror traced the wave patterns onto photosensitive paper wrapped on a drum. Technological developments in electronics have given rise to the higher-precision pendulum seismographs that are widely used today. In these instruments an electric current produced by the motion of the pendulum is passed through electronic circuitry to amplify and digitize the ground motion for more exact readings.

The strength of an earthquake may be measured either by the amount of damage done or through calculations using various instrument readings. The Modified Mercalli Intensity Scale is commonly used to determine the amount of destruction caused by an earthquake. It defines 12 levels of earthquake strength.

The Richter Magnitude Scale is based upon the amount of energy released by the rock movements. The original definition of magnitude in the Richter scale was "the logarithm, to the base 10, of the maximum seismic wave amplitude (in thousandths of a millimeter) recorded on a special seismograph called the Wood-Anderson, at a distance of 62 miles (100 kilometers) from the epicenter. The definition has been extended to permit the use of any calibrated seismograph at any distance.

An earthquake with a Richter magnitude of 2 is about the smallest earthquake that can be felt by humans without instrumental assistance. An increase of one magnitude step corresponds roughly to an increase of 30 times the amount of energy released as

RICHTER SCALE OF EARTHQUAKE MAGNITUDE			
MAGNITUDE LEVEL	**CATEGORY**	**EFFECTS**	**EARTHQUAKES PER YEAR**
less than 1.0 to 2.9	micro	generally not felt by people, though recorded on local instruments	more than 100,000
3.0–3.9	minor	felt by many people; no damage	12,000–100,000
4.0–4.9	light	felt by all; minor breakage of objects	2,000–12,000
5.0–5.9	moderate	some damage to weak structures	200–2,000
6.0–6.9	strong	moderate damage in populated areas	20–200
7.0–7.9	major	serious damage over large areas; loss of life	3–20
8.0 and higher	great	severe destruction and loss of life over large areas	fewer than 3

A birch tree is split by a chasm created when an earthquake struck south-central Alaska, in March 1964. Wilbur E. Garrett/National Geographic Image Collection/Getty Images

seismic waves. Thus, the energy of the great 1964 Alaska earthquake, which had a magnitude of 8.6, was not twice as large as that in a shock of 4.3 magnitude. Rather, it released more than 800,000 times as much energy as one of magnitude 4.3.

However, the Richter scale underestimates the relative size of very large earthquakes. The moment magnitude scale, which takes into account the amount and nature of fault slippage, provides a more consistent measure. (The moment magnitude of the great 1964 Alaska earthquake is 9.2.) Several other magnitude scales also are in use.

PREDICTION

Of the many attempts to find clues for predicting the location, time, and strength of future earthquakes, the best results seem to be associated with seismicity studies using earthquake observatories. Other methods are based on detecting gaps in the seismic record of a region. Segments along a fault where displacement has not taken place for a long time are more likely to release built-up stresses.

Seismologists have found that major earthquakes are often preceded by certain measurable physical changes in the environment around their epicenters. These changes include the degree of crustal deformation in fault zones; the occurrence of dilatancy, that is, an increase in volume, of rocks; and a rise in radon concentrations in wells. Continual monitoring and close scrutiny of these changes are expected to improve prediction capability. Risk maps can be prepared for some earthquake-prone regions,

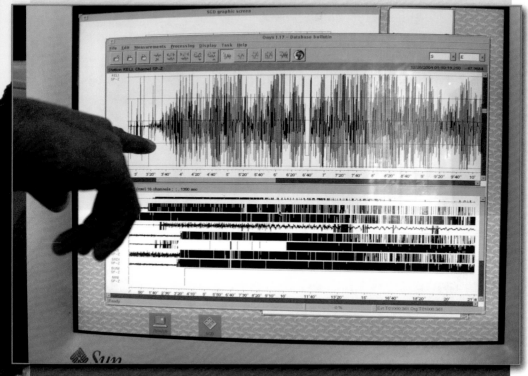

An official points to a seismograph read out on a computer after the Indonesian island of Sumatra was hit by a strong quake on Dec. 26, 2004. Arif Ariadi/AFP/Getty Images

as in California, where surface faults can be monitored. However, this method is not applicable to subduction zones, where seismic activity, generated deep in the Benioff zone, is only vaguely correlated with surface structures.

REDUCING EARTHQUAKE HAZARDS

Although earthquakes can cause death and destruction through such secondary effects as landslides, tsunamis, fires, and fault rupture, the greatest losses in terms of both lives and property usually results from the collapse of man-made surface and subsurface structures during the violent shaking of the ground. Seismologists routinely gather considerable quantities of data to explain the characteristics of the recorded ground motions that take place during earthquakes. Such knowledge is needed to predict ground motions in future earthquakes so that earthquake-resistant structures can be designed.

The most effective way to reduce the destructiveness of earthquakes is to design and construct buildings and other structures capable of withstanding strong shaking. When a site is proposed for the construction

of an office building, for example, factors such as the geometry and frictional properties of a nearby fault line, the passage of seismic waves through surrounding sub-surface rocks, and the condition of the soil and rocks that will be surrounding the building must be considered.

In many cases an accelero-gram, a diagram showing the acceleration of, the velocity of, and the displacement caused by a simulated earthquake, is used to determine the viability of a site for safe building construction. In many countries economic reali-ties usually require that buildings are constructed not for the com-plete prevention of all damage, but to minimize damage from moderate earthquakes and to ensure no major collapse during the strongest earthquakes.

Building knocked off its foundation by the January 1995 earthquake in Kōbe, Japan. **Dr. Roger Hutchison/NGDC**

CHAPTER 4
THE NATURE OF VOLCANOES

Avolcano is a vent, or opening, in Earth's surface through which molten rock, gases, and ash erupt. The word also refers to the form or structure, usually conical, produced by accumulations of erupted material. In some volcanic eruptions the molten rock—called magma when it is underground and lava when it reaches the surface—flows slowly out of the vent. In more violent eruptions lava shoots straight up, and rock fragments are ejected in a great cloud of ash-laden gas that rises high into the air.

Humanity has long been awed by this powerful force of nature. The Romans attributed volcanic events to Vulcan, the god of fire and metalworking. In AD 79 the eruption of Mount Vesuvius destroyed the Roman cities of Pompeii and Herculaneum. Polynesians believe volcanoes to be ruled by the fire goddess Pele. One of the most spectacular volcanic eruptions in recorded

Mount St. Helens volcano, viewed from the south during its eruption on May 18, 1980. © **Getty Images**

history occurred in 1883 with the explosion of Krakatoa, an island in the Sunda Strait near Java. A more recent example from the United States is the dramatic 1980 eruption of Mount St. Helens in the Cascade Range in Washington State.

OCCURRENCE

Volcanoes occur mainly near the boundaries of tectonic plates. They form along belts of tension, where plates diverge, and along belts of compression, where plates converge. Nearly 1,900 volcanoes are active today or are known to have been active in historical times. Of these, almost 90 percent are situated in the Pacific Ring of Fire. The Mediterranean-Asian belt, which accounts for most of the world's earthquakes outside the Ring of Fire, has few volcanoes except for in Indonesia and in the Mediterranean, where they are more numerous. Oceanic volcanoes are strung along the world's oceanic ridges, while the remaining active volcanoes are associated with the Great Rift Valley of East Africa.

Volcanic activity typically alternates between short active periods and much

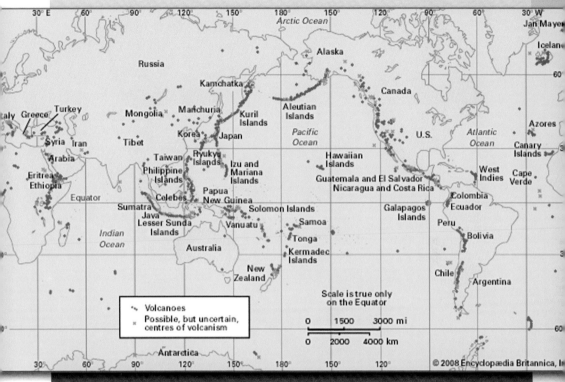

Volcanoes

Possible, but uncertain, centres of volcanism

Scale is true only on the Equator

| 0 | 1500 | 3000 mi |
| 0 | 2000 | 4000 km |

© 2008 Encyclopædia Britannica, Inc.

This map shows volcanoes and thermal fields that have been active during the past 10,000 years. Encyclopædia Britannica, Inc.

longer dormant periods. An extinct volcano is one that is not erupting and is not likely to erupt in the future. A dormant volcano, while currently inactive, has erupted within historic times and is likely to do so in the future. An inactive volcano is one that has not been known to erupt within historic times. Such classification is arbitrary,

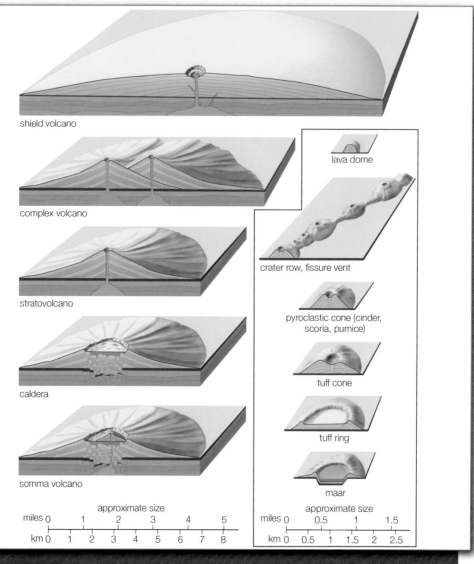

shield volcano

complex volcano

stratovolcano

caldera

somma volcano

lava dome

crater row, fissure vent

pyroclastic cone (cinder, scoria, pumice)

tuff cone

tuff ring

maar

approximate size

miles	0		1		2		3		4		5
km	0	1	2	3	4	5	6	7	8		

approximate size

miles	0	0.5	1	1.5
km	0	0.5 1	1.5 2	2.5

The volcanic landforms shown at left and right are vertically exaggerated, and those shown at right are out of scale to those shown at left. In reality a cinder cone would be approximately one-tenth the size of a stratovolcano. Encyclopædia Britannica, Inc.

however, since almost any volcano is capable of erupting again.

VOLCANIC LANDFORMS

Volcanoes are usually classified by shape and size. These are determined by such factors as the volume and type of volcanic material ejected, the sequence and variety of eruptions, and the environment. Among the most common types are shield volcanoes, stratovolcanoes, and cinder cones.

Shield volcanoes have a low, broad profile created by highly fluid lava flows that spread over wide areas. The lava, usually composed of basalt, cannot build up a cone with sides much steeper than 7 degrees. Over thousands of years, however, these cones can reach massive size. The Hawaiian Islands are composed of shield volcanoes that have built up from the seafloor to the surface some 3 miles (5 kilometers) above. Peaks such as Mauna Loa and Mauna Kea rise to more than 13,600 feet (4,100 meters) above sea level. Hawaii is the largest lava structure in the world, while Mauna Loa, if measured from the seafloor, is the world's largest mountain in terms of both height and volume.

Pahoehoe lava flow, Kilauea volcano, Hawaii, November 1985. J. D. Griggs, U. S. Geological Survey

Stratovolcanoes are the most common volcanic form. They are steep cones composed of alternating layers of lava and pyroclastics, or rock fragments. When a quiet lava flow ends, it creates a seal of solidified lava within the conduit, or channelway, of the volcano. Pressure gradually builds up below, setting the stage for a violent blast of pyroclastic material. These alternating cycles repeat themselves, giving stratovolcanoes a violent reputation.

A cinder cone is a conical hill of mostly cinder-sized pyroclastics. The profile of the cone is determined by the angle of repose—that is, the steepest angle at which debris remains stable and does not slide downhill. Larger cinder fragments, which fall near the summit, can form slopes exceeding 30 degrees. Finer particles are carried farther from the vent and form gentle slopes of about 10 degrees at the base of the cone. These volcanoes tend to be explosive but may also extrude some lava. Cinder cones are numerous, occur in all sizes, and tend to rise steeply above the surrounding area. Those occurring on the flanks of larger volcanoes are called parasitic cones.

MOUNT FUJI

The highest mountain in Japan, Mount Fuji rises to a height of 12,388 feet (3,776 meters) near the Pacific coast of central Honshu, the

largest of the Japanese islands. It is a volcano that has been dormant since its last eruption in 1707 but is still generally classified as active by geologists. The mountain's name, which comes from the language of the indigenous Ainu people, means "everlasting life."

With its graceful conical form, Mount Fuji is a classic stratovolcano. It has become famous throughout the world and is considered the sacred symbol of Japan. Among Japanese there is a sense of personal identification with the mountain, and thousands of Japanese climb to the shrine on its peak every summer. The mountain is the major feature of Fuji-Hakone-Izu National Park.

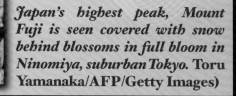

Japan's highest peak, Mount Fuji is seen covered with snow behind blossoms in full bloom in Ninomiya, suburban Tokyo. Toru Yamanaka/AFP/Getty Images)

Other landforms created by volcanoes include craters and calderas. Craters are formed either by the massive collapse of material during volcanic activity, by unusually violent explosions, or later by erosion during dormancy. Calderas are large, basin-shaped depressions. Most of them are formed after a magma chamber drains and no longer supports the overlying cone, which then collapses inward to create the basin. One of the most famous examples is the still-active Kilauea caldera in Hawaii.

CHAPTER 5
VOLCANIC ERUPTIONS

Volcanic eruptions may be violent, even catastrophic, or relatively mild. The most explosive eruptions are essentially blasts of steam that create spectacular displays. Quieter fissure eruptions occur when molten rock pushes through long cracks in Earth's crust and floods the surrounding landscape. Such repeated outpourings of lava can fill surrounding valleys and bury low hills, creating thick lava sequences that eventually become plateaus.

MAGMA

The origin of magma is not clearly understood. About 80 percent of all magma is composed of basalt rock. Geophysical research suggests that volcanic magma forms near the base of Earth's crust and moves upward to a reservoir called a magma chamber before erupting at the surface. Magma rises because it is less dense than the rocks at lower depths, and their heat probably weakens surrounding rocks. The upward movement of magma may also be due to expanding gases within the

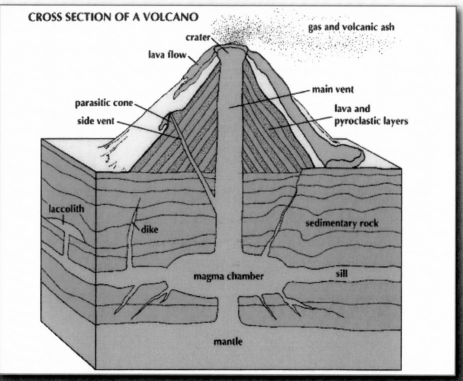

CROSS SECTION OF A VOLCANO

gas and volcanic ash

crater

lava flow

parasitic cone

side vent

main vent

lava and pyroclastic layers

laccolith

dike

sedimentary rock

magma chamber

sill

mantle

In a typical composite volcano hot magma from Earth's mantle rises upward and collects in a magma chamber. As the magma rises it begins to lose gas. During an eruption the magma is forced up through the main vent, or conduit. Lava and pyroclastics are ejected from the crater. Pyroclastics are various-sized particles of hot debris. Usually the lava flows out during the quieter periods. The pyroclastics form when explosions spray out liquid lava, which hardens and settles on the sides of the cone. Water and gases are also ejected. The cone is built up by successive layers of solid lava and pyroclastics. Side vents are formed as the hot lava creeps between the layers of rock or through cracks. When side vents reach the surface, they sometimes form parasitic cones. Sheets of lava that solidify along fissures are called dikes. A laccolith is a mass of solidified magma that intrudes between sedimentary layers and bulges overlying strata. Encyclopædia Britannica, Inc. Copyright Encyclopædia Britannica, Inc.; rendering for this edition by Rosen Educational Services

molten rock or to chemical reactions that dissolve rocks above the magma. Volcanic material moves toward the surface through channelways and is extruded through vents at the surface.

Eruptions take different forms depending on the composition of the magma when it reaches the surface. Sudden eruptions are often associated with low-viscosity (more fluid) magma where the expanding gases form a froth that becomes a light, glassy rock called pumice. In eruptions of high-viscosity (thicker) magmas, the gas pressure shatters the rock into fragments.

LAVA, GAS, AND OTHER HAZARDS

The products of volcanism may be classified into two groups: lava and pyroclastics. Lava is the fluid phase of volcanic activity. Lava usually forms long, narrow rivers of molten rock that flow down the slopes of a volcano. Quieter, more passive eruptions release fluid basalt lava from dikes or dike swarms (magma intrusions that cut across layers of rock). These eruptions cover large areas and often produce ropy lava flows, known by the Hawaiian name pahoehoe. Thicker basalt lava breaks into chunks or

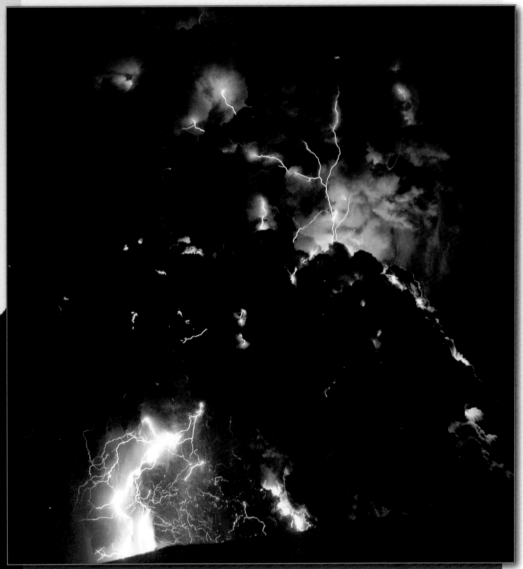

Lightning is seen within a cloud of ash erupting from the Eyjafjallajökull volcano in Southern Iceland, on April 18, 2010. Fearing damage to aircraft and the hazards of flying through the massive ash cloud, many European countries closed their national airspace and grounded flights for several days. Terje Sorgjerd/Getty Images

blocks, forming blocky lava flows, known by the Hawaiian name *aa*. Pyroclastics are various-sized particles of hot debris thrown out of a volcano. Pyroclastic rock fragments, formed by volcanic explosion, are named according to size, with dust as the smallest particles and bombs as the largest. Consolidated ash is called tuff. Whether lava or pyroclastics are being ejected, the eruption is normally accompanied by the expulsion of water and gases, many of which are poisonous.

Styles of eruption and types of lava are associated with different kinds of plate boundaries. Most lavas that come from vents in oceanic divergence zones and from mid-oceanic volcanoes are basaltic. Where ocean plates collide, the rock types basalt and andesite predominate. Near the zone where an ocean plate and a continental plate converge, consolidated ash flows are found.

Explosive eruptions tend to be spectacular events best observed from a safe distance. Earthquakes, high columns of vapors, lightning, and strong whirlwinds often accompany the explosions. The eruption of Krakatoa unleashed a tsunami, a large seismic sea wave, that swept the coasts of Java and Sumatra and drowned more than 36,000 people.

FUMAROLES AND GEYSERS

While a volcano is a vent in Earth's surface from which molten matter, solid rock, and gases erupt, fumaroles and geysers emit only gases and water, respectively. Fumaroles emit water vapor that comes from groundwater heated by magma lying close to the surface.

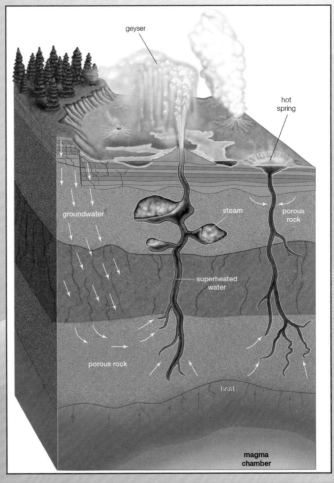

The gases carbon dioxide, sulfur dioxide, and hydrogen sulfide are usually emitted directly from the magma. Fumaroles are often present on active volcanoes during periods of relative quiet between eruptions. Although not violent, fumaroles can be dangerous to humans and animals if noxious fumes are inhaled.

Fumaroles are closely related to hot springs and geysers. A hot spring occurs when groundwater heated by magma comes up through a fracture in the surface. The temperature of the water is substantially higher than the air temperature of the surrounding region. In places where the water table rises near the surface, fumaroles can become hot springs.

Geysers are hot springs with a natural system of plumbing and heating that causes

---

Groundwater percolates through porous rock into fractures deep underground, where heat from a nearby magma chamber superheats the pressurized water to a temperature above the boiling point of water at surface pressure. In hot springs the rising superheated water is cooled below the boiling point by groundwater before reaching the surface. In geysers the superheated water collects in underground pockets. There a small drop in pressure caused by the release of water at the surface flashes the superheated water into steam, which expands and ejects a column of steam and water into the air. When the supply of steam and hot water is exhausted, the spouting stops and the cycle begins again. Encyclopædia Britannica, Inc.

intermittent eruptions of water and steam. The word *geyser* comes from the Icelandic word meaning "to gush." Nearly all the world's true geysers, also known as pulsating springs or gushers, are located in Iceland, New Zealand, and the United States. Both hot springs and geysers are numerous in Yellowstone National Park.

Geysers are known for their often spectacular eruptions that throw water and steam high into the air. No two geysers behave in exactly the same way, and it is very difficult to study the system of underground passages that supplies any one of them. It is believed, however, that the underground structure of a geyser consists of a crooked tubelike opening that leads from the interior to the ground surface. Several small caverns or chambers may be connected to the tube. Groundwater partially fills the tube and some of the connecting caverns. The heated water is trapped under pressure in the crooked tube. Continued heating produces a water temperature above the boiling point, and the steam so produced develops enough pressure to eject a small amount of water to the surface. This expulsion of water in the initial upsurge reduces pressure on the water in the tube. The reduction in pressure causes the remaining water to boil explosively to the point where it drives a column of water and steam, called the geyser jet, into the air. The eruption continues until water and steam are driven out of the tube and storage caverns.

Old Faithful geyser, Upper Geyser Basin, Yellowstone National Park, Wyoming. George Marler/National Park Service

A volcano can grow with frightening speed and often affects territory far beyond the area on which the cone forms. In 2010 the eruption of the Eyjafjallajökull volcano in southern Iceland caused major problems for travelers throughout the world; the volcano produced a huge ash cloud that spread to the east, forcing the closure of many airports across Europe. When volcanoes are

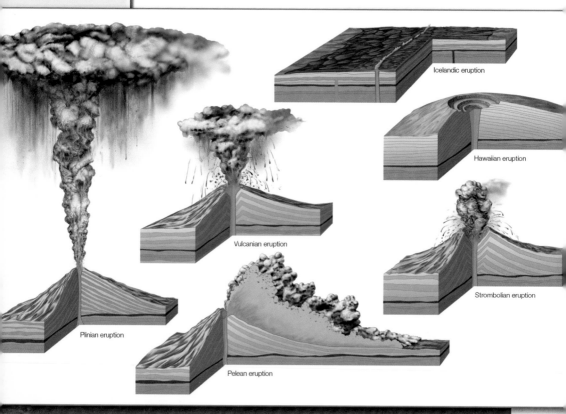

The major types of volcanic eruptions. Encyclopædia Britannica, Inc.

born in the sea, the eruptions may be more violent than those on land because the contact between molten rock and seawater produces steam.

TYPES OF ERUPTIONS

Volcanoes erupt in a wide variety of ways. Even a single volcano may go through several eruption phases in one active period. Eruptions are classified according to the composition and viscosity of the lavas, nature of the flows or ash release, and associated phenomena. Magmatic eruptions are the most common, but the most violent arise from steam explosions when the fiery magma reaches surface water, ice, or groundwater.

Pelean eruptions, named after the 1902 eruption of Mount Pelée on the Caribbean island of Martinique, are characterized by incandescent flows of rock and pumice fragments. The entrapment of high-temperature gases in these "glowing avalanches," known by the French term *nuée ardente*, is associated with a particularly violent phase of eruption.

Eruptions of intermediate force are typified by Plinian eruptions, named after Pliny the Elder, who witnessed the volcanic destruction of Pompeii and Herculaneum.

KRAKATOA

The volcano Krakatoa is located on Rakata, an island in the Sunda Strait between Java and Sumatra, Indonesia. Its eruption in 1883 was one of the most catastrophic ever witnessed in recorded history. Its only known previous eruption was a moderate one in 1680.

On the afternoon of Aug. 26, 1883, the first of a series of increasingly violent explosions occurred. A black cloud of ash rose 17 miles (27 kilometers) above Krakatoa. On the morning of the next day, tremendous explosions were heard 2,200 miles (3,500 kilometers) away in Australia. Ash was propelled to a height of 50 miles (80 kilometers), blocking the Sun and plunging the surrounding region into darkness for two and a half days. The drifting dust caused spectacular red sunsets throughout the following year. Pressure waves in the atmosphere were recorded around the planet, and destructive tsunamis reached as far away as Hawaii and South America. The greatest wave reached a height of 120 feet (36 meters) and took 36,000 lives in the coastal towns of Java and Sumatra. Near the volcano masses of floating pumice, produced from lava cooled in the sea, were thick enough to halt traveling ships.

Everything on the nearby islands was buried under a thick layer of sterile ash. Plant and animal life did not begin to reestablish itself to any degree for five years. The volcano was

quiet until 1927, when a new eruption began. The volcano has been active sporadically since that time, and the cone has continued to grow to an elevation of about 1,000 feet (300 meters) above the sea.

Eruption of Krakatoa in 1960. **Courtesy of the Geological Survey of Indonesia; photograph, D. Hadikusumo**

Plinian eruptions are characterized by both the extrusion of high-viscosity lava flows and the violent explosion of released gases that blast huge quantities of ash, cinders, bombs, and blocks skyward. Volcanic mudflows, landslides, and lahars (flows of volcanic debris) may also follow, particularly if the eruptions are accompanied by rainstorms.

Less violent Hawaiian and Strombolian-type eruptions are associated with fissures that often produce a line of fire fountains. These geyserlike fountains of lava may shoot several hundred feet into the air and form a nearly continuous curtain of fire. The basalt lava is extremely fluid and flows down the mountain sides in torrents. When these streams reach the sea, they form pillow lavas, lobes of stacked lava that resemble a pile of pillows.

STUDY OF VOLCANIC ERUPTIONS

Volcanology, a branch of geology, is the study of volcanoes and volcanic activity. Although volcanoes are difficult to study because of the hazards involved, volcano observatories have existed for decades.

Scientists observe active volcanoes to obtain information that might help predict the timing and intensity of eruptions. Sensitive instruments detect changes in temperature, chemical composition of emissions, Earth movements, magnetic fields, gravity, and other physical properties of the volcano. Modern networks of seismographs provide information on the internal structure and activity of volcanoes. The intensity, frequency, and location of earthquakes provide important clues to volcanic activity, particularly impending eruptions. Movements of magma typically produce numerous tremors, sometimes exceeding 1,000 per day. An almost continuous tremor generally accompanies a lava outpouring. Tiltmeters (instruments that measure tilting of the ground) help detect swelling and deflation of the volcano caused by the accumulation and movement of magma. Researchers also monitor variations in the chemistry and petrology of the lavas and the chemistry of emitted gases.

Conclusion

The introduction of the theory of plate tectonics in the 1960s brought about a scientific revolution. The theory is based on a broad synthesis of geologic and geophysical data and is now almost universally accepted. Incorporating the much older idea of continental drift, plate tectonics has provided an overarching framework for understanding mountain-building processes, earthquakes, and volcanoes. It also provides a way to describe the evolution of Earth's surface and the past geography of continents and oceans. In short, the theory has immensely advanced the scientific understanding of the planet.

While plate tectonics offers an explanation of the causes of earthquakes and volcanoes, geologists study many other aspects of those destructive phenomena as well. Knowledge of natural warning signs, for instance, can help geologists to forecast earthquakes and volcanoes more accurately and thus to minimize damage and save lives.

asthenosphere The layer of Earth's upper mantle lying directly below the lithosphere and composed of partially molten rock.

basalt A hard, dense, dark, often glassy-appearing volcanic rock.

bomb Volcanic fragment larger than 2.5 inches (64 millimeters) in diameter.

convection Heat transfer via movement of liquid or gas.

convergent margin The boundary created between two tectonic plates moving toward each other.

divergent margin Boundary created between two tectonic plates moving apart, where new crust is formed.

epicenter The part of Earth's surface directly above the focus of an earthquake.

extrusion The process of pushing or forcing out.

fault A fracture in Earth's crust.

fumarole Vent in Earth's surface that emits steam and volcanic gas.

lithosphere The rigid outer layer of Earth that includes the crust and outermost mantle is about 60 miles (100 kilometers) thick. It is composed of large and small plates that move and can cause seismic or volcanic activity.

mantle The part of Earth's interior that lies beneath the crust and above the central core.

pyroclastics Hot, solid material ejected into the air during a volcanic eruption.

radon A heavy radioactive gas formed by the decay of radium.

sediment Matter, such as dirt or rocks, that is deposited by water, wind, or glaciers.

seismic Of, subject to, or caused by an earthquake; also of, subject to, caused by, or relating to an earth vibration caused by an earthquake or some other force.

subduction The process in which a denser tectonic plate sinks below another plate and into Earth's mantle as the two plates converge.

tectonic Relating to changes to the structure of a planetary surface.

transform fault Boundary between two plates moving past each other laterally without forming or destroying crust.

trench A long, narrow, and usually steep-sided crack cut into the ocean floor.

tuff Rock composed of volcanic ash that is usually fused together by heat.

Earth Observatory
Earth Observing System Project Science
    Office
Goddard Space Flight Center
Public Inquiries
Mail Code 130
Greenbelt, MD 20771
Web site: http://earthobservatory.nasa.gov
The Earth Observatory features stories,
    maps, images, and news that emerge
    from NASA satellite missions, in-the-
    field research, and climate models.

Earthquakes Canada
Natural Resources Canada
580 Booth
Ottawa, ON K1A 0E4
Canada
(613) 995-0947
Web site: http://earthquakescanada.nrcan.
    gc.ca/index-eng.php
Earthquakes Canada provides informa-
    tion on recent and historic earthquakes
    and earthquake preparation, as well as a
    hazard calculator, seismograph viewer,
    and waveform data. An interactive map
    shows the locations and magnitudes of
    all earthquakes in the past 30 days.

Environmental Protection Agency
Ariel Rios Building
1200 Pennsylvania Avenue NW
Washington, DC 20460
(202) 272-0167
Web site: http://www.epa.gov/
    naturaldisasters
The Environmental Protection Agency
    offers information about and projects
    to promote awareness of preparing
    for and response and recovery after
    natural disasters such as volcanoes and
    earthquakes. It also has webcams of
    important volcanoes such as Mount St.
    Helens and Mount Kilauea.

The Geological Association of Canada
Department of Earth Sciences
Room ER4063, Alexander Murray
    Building
Memorial University of Newfoundland
St. John's, NL A1B 3X5
Canada
(709) 864-7660
Web site: http://www.gac.ca
The Geological Association of Canada is a
    professional organization that publishes
    journals and books, bestows grants and

awards, and encourages lifelong learning in the geological sciences.

National Museum of Natural History
P.O. Box 37012 Smithsonian Inst.
Washington, DC, 20013-7012
Web site: http://www.mnh.si.edu
The National Museum of Natural History
is a part of the Smithsonian Institution,
a world-renowned, state-of-the-art
research center and museum. Students
can visit the site or the museum to inves-
tigate the history of Earth, including
the stones and rocks that make up the
planet itself.

United States Geological Survey
USGS National Center
12201 Sunrise Valley Drive
Reston, VA 20192
(888) 275-8747
Web site: http://www.usgs.gov
The U.S. Geological Survey Web site
includes extensive information about
earthquake and volcano hazards, seismicity and tectonic maps, and many other
resources of interest in relation to the
study of plate tectonics.

WEB SITES

Due to the changing nature of Internet links, Rosen Educational Services has developed an online list of Web sites related to the subject of this book. This site is updated regularly. Please use this link to access the list:

http://www.rosenlinks.com/ies/tect

Chester, Roy. *Furnace of Creation, Cradle of Destruction: A Journey to the Birthplace of Earthquakes, Volcanoes, and Tsunamis* (AMACOM, 2008).

Chippendale, L.A. *The San Francisco Earthquake of 1906* (Chelsea House, 2001).

Federal Emergency Management Agency. *Earthquake Safety Checklist* (FEMA, 2005).

Gallant, R.A. *Plates: Restless Earth* (Benchmark, 2003).

Herbert Howell, Catherine. *Volcano* (National Geographic, 2001).

Jackson, Kay. *Plate Tectonics* (Lucent, 2005).

O'Meara, Donna. *Volcano: A Visual Guide* (Firefly, 2008).

Rubin, Ken. *Volcanoes & Earthquakes* (Simon & Schuster, 2007).

Scarth, Alwyn. *Vulcan's Fury: Man Against the Volcano* (Yale Univ. Press, 2001).

Van Rose, Susanna. *Volcanoes and Earthquakes* (DK, 2008).

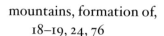